Anthony Neilson

Edward Gant's
Amazing Feats of Loneliness

As transcribed by Mr Anthony Neilson
For the illustrious Theatre Royal, Plymouth
This year of Our Lord, 1881

GW00469180

Methuen Drama

Published by Methuen Drama 2009

1 3 5 7 9 10 8 6 4 2

Methuen Drama
A & C Black Publishers Limited
36 Soho Square
London W1D 3QY
www.methuendrama.com

Edward Gant's Amazing Feats of Loneliness!
first published by Methuen Drama in 2008

Copyright © 2008, 2009 Anthony Neilson

Anthony Neilson has asserted his rights under
the Copyright, Designs and Patents Act, 1988, to be
identified as the author of this work

ISBN 978 1 408 11952 5

A CIP catalogue record for this book is available from
the British Library

Typeset by Country Setting, Kingsdown, Kent CT14 8ES
Printed and bound in Great Britain by
CPI Cox and Wyman, Reading RG1 8EX

The Nuffield
southampton

Headlong

Headlong Theatre
and the
Nuffield Theatre, Southampton
present

Edward Gant's AMAZING Feats of Loneliness

by Anthony Neilson

This play was first performed at The Drum Theatre
at the Theatre Royal, Plymouth, on 6th May 2002.

This production was first performed at
The Nuffield Theatre, Southampton, on 26th February 2009.

Edward Gant's Amazing Feats of Loneliness

by Anthony Neilson

NICHOLAS LUDD	**Paul Barnhill**
JACK DEARLOVE	**Sam Cox**
MADAME POULET	**Emma Handy**
EDWARD GANT	**Simon Kunz**

Director	**Steve Marmion**
Designer	**Tom Scutt**
Lighting Designer	**Malcolm Rippeth**
Composer & Sound Designer	**Tom Mills**
Casting Director	**Julia Horan**
Assistant Director	**Jack McNamara**

Production Manager	**Matt Noddings**
Company Stage Manager	**Nick Hill**
Deputy Stage Manager	**Rebecca James**
Assistant Stage Manager	**Sam Orme**
Costume Supervisor and Wardrobe Manager	**Antonia Rudgard**
Production LX/Re-Lighter	**Joe Kennion**
Set Build	**RK Resources**
Set Transport	**Southern Van Lines**
Lighting Hires	**Hawthorn Theatrical**
Production Insurance	**Giles Insurance**
Press	**Cliona Roberts** (0207 704 6224, cliona@crpr.co.uk)
Production Photography	**Manuel Harlan**
Graphic Design	**Eureka!** (www.eureka.co.uk)

With thanks to: Molly Einchcomb, Max Humphries, National Youth Theatre, Jenny Lee and Jag Props

Cast

PAUL BARNHILL (NICHOLAS LUDD)

Training: East 15 and Salford College.

Theatre: includes *Antony and Cleopatra, Julius Ceasar, The Tempest, Twelfth Night* (RSC); *The Merchant of Venice, Anna Karenina* (Bolton Octagon); *Flamingoland, The Bat, East Lynne, Romeo and Juliet, Kes* (New Vic Theatre); *King Cotton* (The Lowry/Liverpool Empire); *Much Ado About Nothing* (Sheffield Crucible); *Faustus* (Northampton Theatre Royal); *The Merchant of Venice, Henry V, A Woman Killed With Kindness, Antony and Cleopatra* (Northern Broadsides); *Search and Destroy* (New End Hampstead); *Death of a Salesman, The Nativity, Whisper of Angels Wings, Julius Ceasar, All That Trouble That We Had* (Birmingham Rep); *All's Well That Ends Well* (Nuffield Southampton); *Tom Jones* (Theatr Clwyd); *Taking Liberties* (Chester Gateway Theatre); *Hamlet* (National Studio).

West End: *Die Fledermaus* (Sadlers Wells); *Pirates of Penzance* (Queens Theatre); *Yeoman of the Guard* (The Savoy); *RSC Season* (Novello).

Televison: includes *Holby City, Doctors, The Real Arnie Griffen, The Fabulous Bagel Boys, Peak Practice* and the racist villain Josh Carter in *Brookside.*

Film: *Anorak of Fire* and Mike Leigh's *Topsy Turvy.*

Writing Credits: Comedies- *Edge Falls* (series 1 and 2); *The Spaceship* (series 1 and 2); *Beyond The Pole, Beyond the Back of Beyond, Casualties, Bloody Rough Holiday Guide* (BBC); *Flyfishing* (Shooting Pictures). *Tourist Guide to the B5053* (New series for Radio 4 recording in July).

SAM COX (JACK DEARLOVE)

Theatre: includes *Oedipus, The UN Inspector* (National); *So Close to Home* (Arcola); *On Religion* (British Council); *Shrieks of Laughter* (Soho Theatre); *Tintin* (Barbican); *Festen* (Almeida/West End); *Serjeant Musgrave's Dance* (OSC); *Great Expectations* (Bristol Old Vic); *Arabian Night* (ATC/Soho Theatre); *The Power of Darkness, The Revengers Tragedy* (Orange Tree); *Sweet Dreams* (Sphinx Theatre Company); *A Doll's House* (Birmingham Rep); *Uncle Silas* (Lyric Hammersmith/Tour); *Dearly Beloved* (Hampstead/Tour); *A Bright Room Called Day* (Bush); *Insignificance, The Ruling Class* (Liverpool Playhouse); *Run for your Wife* (West End); *Macbeth, The Jail Diary of Albie Sachs* (Young Vic); *Jesus Christ*

Superstar, Jeeves, Joseph and the Amazing Technicolour Dreamcoat (West End); *God in Ruins, Macbeth, King John, Henry V, Romeo and Juliet, Richard II, Troilus and Cressida* (RSC).

Television: includes *The Commander, Inspector Lynley Mysteries, Suitable Vengeance, Doctor Who III, Doctor Who II, The Last Will and Testament of Billy Two Sheds, Holby City, The Murder of Stephen Lawrence, The Wings of Angels, London Bridge, Peak Practice, Crime Traveler, Madson, Back Up, Prime Suspect, Kavanagh QC, The Chief, Dandelion Dead, The Bill, Foreign Affairs, The Orchid House, Die Kinder, Bergerac, Blind Justice, Dead Head, McKenzie, The Chinese Detective, Fords on Water.*

Film: includes *Agora, Hippie Hippie Shake, Double Heartbeat, Call at Corazon, Burnt Fen.*

Radio: includes *Festen* (BBC).

EMMA HANDY (MADAME POULET)

Training: LAMDA

Theatre: includes *Crown Matrimonial* (ACT); *A Midsummer Night's Dream; Vincent in Brixton* (National/West End); *50 Revolutions* (Trafalgar Studios); The *Merchant of Venice, Bad Weather, Twelfth Night* (RSC); *The Wood Demon* (Playhouse); *Csongor Es Tunde* (Merlin International, Budapest).

Television: includes *Wire in the Blood 2, 3, 4, 5, 6, Silent Witness, Beneath the Skin, William and Mary 2, Hear the Silence, The Bill, Real Crime, Emma Brody, See Me, Innocents, Black Cab, Pretending to be Judith* .

Film: includes *Vincent in Brixton, Vacuums, Iris, Club le Monde, Velvet Goldmine.*

SIMON KUNZ (EDWARD GANT)

Theatre: includes *King Lear, As You Like It* (OSC); *Don Gil of the Green Breeches, Madness in Valencia* (Gate Theatre); *Richard III, Napoli Milionaria* (National); *Live like Pigs* (Royal Court); *The Park* (RSC); *Mojo* (Duke of York's); *The House of Correction* (The Wrestling School); *The Caretaker* (Bristol Old Vic).

Television: includes *Secret Diary of a Call Girl, Poppy Shakespeare, Trial and Retribution, Al Murray's Multiple Personality Disorder, Hustle, In This Life, Lock Stock, Brass Eye, Hippies, Harry Enfield and*

Chums, My Family, Spaced, Oliver Twist, Scarlet Pimpernell, Auf Wiedersehen Pet, Waking the Dead, Blackbeard, The Abolition of Slavery, Greenwing, Nostradamus, The Fall of Rome, Magnolia, Coronation Street.

Film: includes Four Weddings and a Funeral, Young Poisoners, Golden Eye, The Parent Trap, The Bunker, Affair of the Necklace, Cave, Matchpoint, January 2nd, I Could Never Be Your Woman, Desaccord Parfait, City of Ember.

Creative Team

ANTHONY NEILSON (Writer)

Theatre: includes Welfare my Lovely (Traverse Theatre); Normal (Edinburgh Festival/Finborough Arms); Penetrator (Edinburgh Festival/Finborough/ Royal Court Upstairs); The Year of the Family (Finborough); The Censor (Finborough/Royal Court, which won the Writers Guild Award for Best Fringe Play 1997); Realism (Edinburgh International Festival/Lyceum Theatre); God in Ruins (RSC); Relocated (Royal Court).

Other Theatre: includes Edward Gant's Amazing Feats of Loneliness (Plymouth Theatre Royal); Stitching (Traverse/Bush/UK Tour for which he was nominated Evening Standard 'Most Promising Newcomer' 2002); The Lying Kind (Jerwood Theatre/Royal Court); The Wonderful World of Dissocia (Tron/Royal Lyceum Edinburgh/Plymouth Theatre Royal/Royal Court).

Film: includes The Debt Collector which Anthony wrote and directed. It was released in 1999 (Dragon Pictures/Film 4) and won the Fipresci International Critics Award at the Troia International Film Festival in the same year.

As Director only: includes The Death of Klinghoffer (Edinburgh International Festival/Scottish Opera), which won a Herald Angel Award, Jeffrey Dahmer is Unwell (King's Head, Islington).

Anthony is currently under commission to Stone City/BBC4 for a 90-minute film. He will direct a production of The Drunks for the RSC in 2009 and his new play The Séance will premiere as part of the National Theatre's Connections season. Anthony is currently Literary Associate of the RSC.

STEVE MARMION (Director)

Steve directed Headlong Theatre's production of Faustus at Richmond Theatre and on a UK Tour.

Recent Theatre: includes *Metropolis* (Theatre Royal Bath); *Only The Brave* (Edinburgh Festival); *Vincent River* (Brits Off Broadway Festival, New York).

Other Theatre: includes *Team Spirit* (National/Plymouth Theatre Royal); *A Date To Remember* (Little Theatre Company/Soho Studio); *SK8, Multiplex* (Plymouth Theatre Royal); *Sleeping Beauty, Miranda's Magic Mirror, Tiny Tales* (Stephen Joseph Theatre); *Lock Up* (Educational Project, National Theatre); *Tempest 2000* (Sherman Theatre); *Caliban's Island* (Touched Theatre/UK Tour/Edinburgh Festival); *97 – Hillsborough* (Ugly Theatre/UK Tour/Edinburgh Festival); *Ghetto* (Hertfordshire County Youth Theatre, Watford); *Little Nell, Images of a Lonely Poets War* (East 15); *Lunchtime Lottery* (Plush Productions, Covent Garden Studio). For the London One Act Theatre Festival, he directed *Mad Margaret's Revenge* (also Edinburgh Festival), which won the 'Best New Play Award' and *Madam Butterfly's Child*, which won the 'Best Overall Production Award' (also Pleasance Theatre/Greenwich Festival/Hong Kong International Festival/Edinburgh Festival).

Steve transferred Rupert Goold's production of *Macbeth* to Broadway and was an assistant and then an Associate Director with the RSC for two years between 2006-07. He has directed workshops for the National Theatre, Hampstead Theatre, the Royal Court and the RSC (with whom he is an Education Associate Practitioner).

TOM SCUTT (Designer)

Training: Royal Welsh College, first class honours degree in Theatre Design.

For his work with Headlong Theatre, Tom was awarded the 2007 Linbury Biennial Prize and the Jocelyn Herbert Award for Stage Design.

Theatre: includes *The Merchant of Venice* (Octagon Theatre, 2008 Manchester Evening News 'Best Design' nomination); *Unbroken, The Internationalist* (Gate Theatre); *Metropolis* (Theatre Royal Bath); *The Observer* (as design consultant, National Studio); *Paradise Lost* (Southwark Playhouse); *Mad Funny Just* (winner of the 2008 'Old Vic New Voices Award'); *The Water Harvest* (Theatre 503); *Return* (Watford); *Comedy of Errors* (RSC Swan); *Skellig* (OnO Productions tour); *Loaded* (Fireraisers Theatre); *Branwen* (Wales Millenium Centre); *Dog Tags* (European Live Arts Network).

Current Designs: include *Bay* (Young Vic).

MALCOLM RIPPETH (Lighting Designer)

For Headlong: *Six Characters in Search of an Author* (Chichester Festival Theatre/West End) and *Faustus* (Hampstead Theatre/UK tour).

Other Theatre: includes *Calendar Girls* (Chichester Festival Theatre/UK Tour/West End); *Don John* (Kneehigh/RSC); *Brief Encounter* (Kneehigh/ West End/UK Tour); *His Dark Materials* (Birmingham Rep/West Yorkshire Playhouse); *Cymbeline, Nights at the Circus, The Bacchae* (Kneehigh); *Mary Rose* (Edinburgh Lyceum); *Kafka's Dick* (Watford); *The Grouch, Scuffer, The Lion, the Witch and the Wardrobe, Homage to Catalonia* (West Yorkshire Playhouse); *Tutti Frutti* (National Theatre of Scotland); *James and the Giant Peach* (Northampton); *Trance* (Bush); *Cyrano de Bergerac* (Bristol Old Vic); *Someone Else's Shoes, Mother Courage* (ETT); *The Bloody Chamber, The Little Prince* (Northern Stage); *Hamlet* (ETT/West End).

Opera, musical and dance work includes *Carmen Jones* (Royal Festival Hall); *Seven Deadly Sins* (WNO/Diversions Dance); *The Philosophers' Stone* (Garsington Opera); and numerous productions for balletLORENT, most recently *Designer Body* and *MaEternal*.

TOM MILLS (Composer and Sound Designer)

Tom is a musician and composer, and occasionally works with video, film and producing live shows, online documentaries and blogs. He plays bass guitar, double bass and sings backing vocals in Brighton-based band *Passenger* and works as a session musician. As a pit musician Tom has worked on *Nunsense* (Nuffield Theatre); *Les Miserables* (Zenith, Bath); *Hot Mikado* (Bristol Music Club); *Little Shop of Horrors* (V2 Productions); *Grease* (KYT); *Oliver* (BAOS, Bristol) and *Godspell* (Susan Nash/Bristol).

As Composer and Sound Designer: *Unbroken* (Gate Theatre); *Metropolis* (Theatre Royal, Bath); *Othello* (Assembly Rooms, Bath), *Three Amigos The Musical, Assassins* (Eyebrow Productions).

As Actor/Musician: *The Good Person of Szechwan*, *The Berlin Cabaret* (Theatre Royal, Bath).

As Musical Director: *Return to the Forbidden Planet* (Bath Spa Music Society); *Band of Blues Brothers* (Panthelion Productions).

Headlong

Headlong Theatre is dedicated to new ways of making theatre. By exploring revolutionary writers and practitioners of the past and commissioning new work from artists from a wide variety of backgrounds we aim constantly to push the imaginative boundaries of the stage. Under the Artistic Directorship of Rupert Goold (Olivier Award winner for Best Director, 2008), Headlong makes exhilarating, provocative and spectacular new work to take around the country and around the world.

'The country's most exciting touring company'
Daily Telegraph

'Wild, mad and deeply intelligent theatre'
Sunday Times

'Rupert Goold is one of the most exciting young talents in British theatre today'
Times

Headlong Theatre is:

Artistic Director	Rupert Goold
Executive Producer	Henny Finch
Acting Executive Producer	Greg Ripley-Duggan
Finance Manager	Julie Renwick
Literary Associate	Ben Power
Assistant Producer	Jenni Kershaw
Administrative Assistant	Lindsey Alvis

www.headlongtheatre.co.uk

info@headlongtheatre.co.uk

The Nuffield Southampton

*'I'd happily walk the distance to The Nuffield Theatre, Southampton,
if everything that lay in wait was anything like as good as
Patrick Sandford's revival of A Streetcar Named Desire'*
Daily Telegraph, May 2008

The Nuffield Theatre, situated on the University of Southampton's campus, is one of the South's leading producing theatres. Originally opened by the University of Southampton in 1964, The Nuffield Theatre became an independent charitable trust in 1982, funded by Arts Council England, Southampton City Council, Hampshire County Council and the University of Southampton.

Over the last forty years The Nuffield has come to be recognised in England and abroad as a major force in British Theatre. Today, The Nuffield led by its Artistic Director, Patrick Sandford, creates award-winning productions that tour nationally and sometimes internationally.

The theatre also plays host to the world's best national and international touring companies and regularly attracts some of the country's most gifted and well-regarded actors. Visiting shows this season include Théâtre des Bouffes du Nord and Cheek by Jowl's highly acclaimed production of *Andromaque* by Jean Racine, Out of Joint's Australian co-production of *The Convict's Opera* and European circus troupe Circo de la Sombra, amongst others.

The Nuffield has become a vital artistic resource for Southampton and the surrounding area, and invests in developing new artists and productions and provides a full and varied educational and participatory programme. The Nuffield also runs a highly acclaimed writers' group for aspiring playwrights and is home to Hampshire Youth Theatre.

In 2007 the Company won a tender to run a programme of theatre, dance, music, cabaret and comedy in two theatres in a new arts complex due to open in 2014 in the Guildhall Square in Southampton. This marks a significant expansion for the Company which will also continue to operate its existing theatre as a producing house.

**For more information on what's happening at The Nuffield
this season please contact the box office on 023 8067 1771
or log onto the website www.nuffieldtheatre.co.uk**

Edward Gant's
Amazing Feats of Loneliness

As transcribed by Mr Anthony Neilson
For the illustrious Theatre Royal, Plymouth
This year of Our Lord, 1881

Edward Gant's Amazing Feats of Loneliness! was first performed at the Drum Theatre, Plymouth, on 13 May 2002. The cast was as follows:

Christine Entwisle	Madame Poulet
Stuart McQuarrie	Edward Gant
Matthew Pidgeon	Nicholas Ludd
Barney Power	Jack Dearlove

Director Anthony Neilson
Designer Bob Bailey
Lighting Designer Chahine Yavroyan
Sound Designer Matt Dando

The Players

Edward Gant   Himself
Opium Den Client
The Phantom of the Dry
Madame Poulet   Sanzonetta Tutti
Louisa Von Kettelmein-
    Kurstein Frond
Bear One
Herself
Jack Dearlove   The Doctor
A Pimple
Salvatore Avaricci
Edgar Thomas Dawn
Bear Two
Himself
Nicholas Ludd   Campanetti Tutti
A Pimple
Ranjeev the Uncomplicated
Himself

Notes

The above castings, the transcript that follows and all stage directions therein are as accurate to the event witnessed as the transcriber's memory allows. In any further recreation of this extraordinary evening, all may be seen as moveable (where it is less than ludicrous to do so). These short histories may also be of use . . .

Madame Poulet was so known on account of her career previous to joining Mr Gant's troupe, wherein she took the aspect of a chicken and somehow simulated the actual laying of eggs. She took this act and, indeed, all her parts quite seriously and seemed, to the observer, to exist in a world of her own making. Gant seemed to have a peculiar fondness for her, though this is but conjecture on my part.

'Little' Nicky Ludd took to the stage as a child, most popularly impersonating a young Highland lassie.

Unfortunately, he carried on this act long beyond it was seemly to do so, wherein he fell upon hard and notorious times. Exploited by a radical political body, he was rescued by Mr Gant just as he was about to perpetrate a great and murderous treason upon the State. By the time of the evening transcribed, fuelled by rumours of a new theatrical realism in the East, he seemed to me disillusioned with Mr Gant and his methods. The animosity this engendered seemed most overtly directed towards Jack Dearlove, whose authoritarian nature appeared to inflame him.

Sgt Jack Dearlove, alongside Edward Gant, survived the infamous Charge of the Light Brigade. He believed that Gant had dragged him to safety that fateful day though – having been temporarily blind at the time – the veracity of this was never established beyond question. It hardly mattered, as Dearlove was devoted to the notion of service, and this perceived debt gave focus to his life. His immaculate devotion to Gant stretched from the earliest days of Gant's Midget Opera to the performance here transcribed. He was, as noted, at odds with Mr Ludd, whose notion of social enlightenment and insolent attitude towards Mr Gant embodied all he despised in the youth of the day.

I know not what became of the members of this troupe but dearly hope they are at peace, wherever they may be. I was but a lad when I witnessed the events herein, and set them down in the hope that their endeavours may echo beyond my own demise; I do so with thanks, for one of the two most astonishing evenings of my life so far . . .

Act One

Darkness . . .

Gant
> My good and pure ladies
> My brave and gentle men
> BEHOLD (if you will)
> The Oceanic Planet Earth!

Above us, the underside of a globe.

Behold the firmament's most precious jewel, around which does revolve all the bodies of the Heavens

One by one, the performers enter. Each carries a long stick, atop which sway representations of the following. In procession, they circle the suspended globe.

> The Moon – la Luna.
> The Sun – le Soleil.
> The war planet Mars.
> The ringed planet Saturn.

Each performer, in turn, takes the light for his or her introduction.

The Moon held aloft by the heavenly Madame Poulet . . .

The Sun borne defiantly by our own Mr Nicholas Ludd . . .

And struggling bravely with both Mars and Saturn, my steadfast Sergeant, Jack Dearlove . . .

The last of them exits. **Mr Gant** *is revealed.*

And holding the planets fast, to night's velvet train, the silverpin points we call THE STARS!

He throws up a handful of glitter, which catches the light and rains back down to earth.

Now let it come down, this watery world! *The globe shudders but does not move.*

Now let it COME DOWN, this watery world!

The sound of a winch. Creakily, the globe winds downwards.

And let us (if we dare) take the aspect of God, gazing down (as does he) on this most various of his creations.

The descended globe is revealed as flat on top. Britain dominates the relief map: a naive, imperialist view of the world, bristling with Union Jacks.

Gant   A world of water, yes, but of many climates also: of sand and ice and trees and grass; of mountain, field and cloud. And on this Earth a billion creatures live, but most uniquely Man, who differs from all other beasts in one important way . . .

For while the beasts can be divided into those that form societies and those which bide alone 'tis only Man bestrides the two.

On the one hand, his great success has come about through partnership, and common effort –

Dearlove *and* **Ludd** *shake hands to illustrate this, while* **Madame Poulet** *acts out laying flowers on a grave to illustrate what follows.*

Gant   – yet, on the other, he has been gifted (or cursed) with the absolute knowledge of his mortality – and here his true uniqueness lies.

All three enact a hunting scene.

The beast senses danger at the *moment* it arises and forgets it the moment it has passed. But Man – Man lives in its shadow all the time. *He knows that he will die –*

Madame Poulet *falls.*

Gant   – and it is this terrifying fact –

Dearlove, *also, falls.*

Gant   – that imprisons each man within his own mind. And thus the most sociable of God's creations is far the most alone.

He taps his cane and the players exit.

Ladies and gentleman, as some of you may know, my name is Edward Gant: prodigy, soldier, traveller, poet – but always and ever a showman. As such, it has been my mission to bring you the most wonderous and bizarre that the world has to offer.

But what I bring you now is no mere freak show. You will gasp, yes, and you will marvel and you will see your share of grotesquerie. But the deformities on show this evening are not the deformities of the frame, but those of the heart and mind.

I have scoured every continent to find these most astonishing testaments. Alas, I cannot put before you the subjects themselves, but I will – with the help of my players – attempt to represent their tales to you as truly as time and talent will allow.

So without further ado, I present for your astonishment the Extraordinary! The Terrible! The AMAZING FEATS OF LONELINESS!

An explosion! And **Gant** *disappears.*

*

Ludd *and* **Dearlove** *enter, kicking the show off with a song.*

Ludd *sings and plays, hardly concealing his irritation at* **Dearlove**'s *banal accompanying illustrations . . .*

Ludd
    Ladies and gentlemen,
    Kindly let me address
    The first of our stories
    Of heartbreak and loneliness.
    Tragic, it may be,
    Sad and bizarre, but still
    We've added a dash of humour
    In the hope it will sweeten the pill.

Our story takes place
In the country we know as Italy,
The Southernmost part at that
In the region surrounding Sicily.
Imagine the sunshine,
Imagine the grapes on the vine,
The smell of bread baking,
The making and drinking of wine

At this point, **Ludd** *surreptitiously remonstrates with* **Dearlove,** *attempting to halt his actions. This only partially succeeds:* **Dearlove** *continues his actions behind* **Ludd**'s *back.*

Ludd
But first let us travel
To Italy's capital Rome,
Where Mr Edward Gant
Had the fortune to own a small home.
He can never return there,
If he does it's the end of his world,
His one souvenir
Is the tale you'll now hear –
Sanzonetta, the Pimple-Faced Girl!

The two exit, and we can see that they will be having words backstage.

Madame Poulet, *in character, is now on stage, crying softly.*
Gant *enters.*

Gant   Just as a mother cannot ignore her baby's cry, no gentleman can happily pass a weeping woman. And so I found myself by the La Trevi fountain one winter, offering solace to a girl with a pockmarked face . . .

*

Girl   You are kind, Sir, to sit with me in the cold.

Gant   Not at all, my dear. It is no burden to sit with a beautiful girl.

Girl   You needn't humour me. I know I am not that.

Gant   Perhaps I see deeper than your tortured skin.

Girl   Then you are kinder still and I must reward you.

She hands him a pearl necklace.

It is all I have to give.

Gant   My dear girl – I cannot accept this –

Girl   You must. There is little enough kindness in the world. It should be rewarded when it occurs.

Gant   But this is a valuable thing. Is it not precious to you? Besides, I hardly think the Italians are ready for a man in jewellery.

Girl   Is there no special lady in your life? Give it her, with my blessing.

Gant   There are many ladies in my life.

Girl   Then give them one each!

She unloads a heap of them into his hands.

Gant   Are they imitations?

Girl   No, Sir, they are not.

Pause.

Gant   Do you mean they are stolen? Tell me you are not a thief.

Girl   They are real, Sir, and I am very far from a thief. But I have been much stolen from.

Gant   Intrigued, I pressed her further and she revealed to me then the extraordinary events of her life . . .

Her name was Sanzonetta Tutti and she was one of two sisters born to modest society. A normal girl in childhood, from the age of fourteen she was afflicted by severe attacks of pimples.

She was subject to ridicule, of course; but, to make matters worse, her sister, Campanetti had blossomed into the most gorgeous womanhood . . .

*

Campanetti *flounces in with a bouquet of flowers.*

Campanetti   My, but I am tired of these suitors!

Sanzonetta   Which one was that?

Campanetti   Guffini, the librarian's son.

Sanzonetta   I thought you said he was nice.

Campanetti   The backwards are often nice; they haven't the wit to be nasty.

Sanzonetta   The flowers are well chosen.

Campanetti   Which proves my point: were he as wise as he is ugly, he'd have brought a pig's arse and perhaps gained in the comparison!

Pause.

There is so much stress involved in choosing a husband! Especially now you have become ugly: all Papa's expectations are shouldered by me alone. Sometimes I envy you, Sanzonetta. It must be curiously restful, knowing no one would touch you with a gondolier-pole.

Pause.

My goodness; the shadows thrown by your pimple-heads show it has gone six o'clock! Mashetti, the horse-butcher's son is due to call at seven; I must prepare.

Oh, and Sanzonetta, I do not wish to be cruel but – should you answer the door to him – would you mind putting a bucket over your head, lest he spill his guts on the marbling?

Pause. **Sanzonetta** *nods.*

Campanetti   You are a darling!

*

Gant   Campanetti could not have known the agony her careless remarks caused her sister.

Sanzonetta had tried everything to cure her affliction; taken every remedy, seen every doctor, adopted any habit that might lessen the attacks. There was every chance the condition would pass in time; the danger was that it would leave her –

*

The **Doctor** *enters.*

Doctor   – irreversibly scarred!

Sanzonetta   Scarred? You mean – for ever?

Doctor   It stands to reason, Signora; your skin bubbles hot like a cauldron. If this should persist for long enough then, yes, of course – it will scar you.

Sanzonetta   Is there no way I can avoid this fate?

Doctor   Fate cannot be avoided, Sanzonetta. That's why they call it fate.

Pause.

However, you can take care not to exacerbate the condition.

Take for instance, the boy who compared your face to a pizza. Cruel words, yes, but not wholly inaccurate. Each one of your tomato-red pimples contains a substance not unlike melted mozzarella. It is this that gives them their eye-catching white points. Now – if you apply sufficient pressure to these pimples, they will rupture, expelling their cheese in an often quite dramatic fashion.

Sanzonetta   No – how disgusting!

Doctor   Disgusting, yes, but you may also find the sensation of – ejaculation – strangely satisfying. Do not underestimate its allure; you rupture one, then another and soon the pimples will be singing to you, luring you as if hypnotised. 'Squeeze us,' they will sing. 'Expel our sweet cheese! Squeeze us!'

You must deny them, Sanzonetta! Their song serves only to lure you to the rocks! No matter how tempted you are, you must close your ears, strap down your hands, resist, resist!

Sanzonetta   Yes, I will!

Doctor   And come back in a month.

*

Gant   Sanzonetta was as good as her word – at first. But the doctor also spoke the truth. The song of the pimples sounded louder every day . . .

Sanzonetta *tosses and turns in her bed.*

Pimples (*sing*)
  Squeeze us, Sanzonetta –
  Expel our cheese – squeeze us . . .

Sanzonetta   No, I won't – I won't – !

The song grows louder and louder.

No – please – I don't want to be scarred – !

The song reaches a pitch and she jumps out of bed.

Yes! All right! I will do what you ask! But cease your endless song!

She runs to the mirror.

Gant   Wretched and broken, Sanzonetta chose the most taut and swollen pimple on her once lovely face. She pressed her knuckles to it, either side, and applied all her strength to its stubborn core.

The **Pimples** *moan, ever more frenzied: 'Yes, yes, yes!'*

She felt the pressure build and build – felt the tiny hairline cracks split across her tightening skin, her knuckles whitening with the strain and then – AND THEN – AND THEN – !

The **Pimples** *reach a pitch.* **Sanzonetta** *cries out and then –*

A tiny pearl rolls across the floor.

Pause. She picks it up, studies it, smells it.

Campanetti *enters.*

Campanetti   What is all this commotion, Sanzonetta?! You know I need my beauty sleep!

Pause.

What is that you have there?

Sanzonetta   Nothing . . .

Campanetti   Let me see. Sanzonetta – Sanzonetta!

Sanzonetta *gives her the pearl.*

Campanetti   Where did you get this? Did you steal this from my box?

Sanzonetta   No, I swear!

Campanetti   Don't lie to me, sister. Where else would you come upon a pearl such as this? It is certain no gentleman gave it you.

Sanzonetta   It is no pearl, Campanetti.

Campanetti   What do you take me for? You think I do not know a pearl when I see it? And a quite exquisite one at that . . . Come now, confess. Where did this come from, if not from my box?

Sanzonetta   It came from – my face.

Campanetti   From your face? Have you gone mad, Sanzonetta?

Sanzonetta   No, truly, I –

Campanetti   For either you believe it yourself or you believe that I will believe; and each of these is clearly madness.

Sanzonetta   I am as disbelieving as you, my sister, but I swear it; I attempted to squeeze one of my pimples and that is what came forth.

Pause.

Campanetti   Show me, then.

Sanzonetta   I will try.

She tries again, groaning with the effort.

Campanetti   This had best be no trick, sister; for it is quite the most revolting thing to witness!

With a final squeal, another pearl pops out and rolls across the floor. **Campanetti** *picks it up and studies it. She looks at her sister, amazed.*

Campanetti   It's a pearl!

Sanzonetta   I know.

Campanetti   It came from your face!

Sanzonetta   I know!

Pause.

Campanetti   Do you realise what this means?! If each of your pimples harbours a pearl of this perfection?!

Sanzonetta *shakes her head.*

Campanetti   It means that we are rich, my sister! It means that we are rich!

*

Gant   The sun was dawning by the time Sanzonetta had forced the last pearl from her ravaged, bloody face. This crop alone would have been sufficient to raise them into the lower ranks of privilege, but – to Campanetti's delight – a day later, her sister's face was once more in bloom.

Within months, Campanetti had established a thriving business, trading in pearls of such quality that the Tutti name was soon famous the length and breadth of Europe. Their newfound wealth allowed the two sisters to acquire a substantial country home in Sicily.

But – while Campanetti lived the high-life – Sanzonetta's circumstances had hardly improved . . .

*

Campanetti *enters, dripping with pearl jewellery.*

Campanetti   Sanzonetta – what are you doing in the sunlight? You know production slows in the sunlight!

Sanzonetta   But it is damp in the cellar.

Campanetti   I know, my dear. But we must satisfy this Parisian order; they have paid us handsomely for a prompt delivery.

Sanzonetta   You mean they have paid you handsomely.

Campanetti   I mean what I said, my sister. Your share of the proceeds lies in your account.

Sanzonetta   Exactly; and it will continue to lie there, as I am never allowed the time to spend it!

Campanetti   I sympathise, my dear, I do. But only God knows how long your bounteous condition will continue. We must take advantage while we can. Your day will come, my sister.

Sanzonetta   Easy for you to say; it would seem your day is upon you and has been for many a month.

Campanetti   Sanzonetta – I have just this moment returned from Spain. In the morning, I set sail for England. What more can I do than play my part?

Sanzonetta   You could begin by changing the name of our company.

Campanetti *(sighs)*   Sanzonetta –

Sanzonetta   I know you will say you are protecting me, but I do not see how it protects me to name it The Campanetti Pearl Company.

Campanetti   It is a matter of convenience, nothing more.

Sanzonetta   So you say. But, sister – I never see the wonder on the client's faces, never see my pearls adorn their necks. Why should I also be so disavowed? Why can it not be known that I am the source of these wonderful pearls?

Campanetti   Don't be a fool, Sanzonetta; you think the great and good would be so keen to wear our pearls if they knew they came from a teenager's face? No – the truth would ruin our business and do you no credit, either. At the moment, people merely think you ugly; would you prefer that they deride you as a freak?

Reluctantly, **Sanzonetta** *shakes her head.*

Campanetti   Then you have your answer.

Pause. **Sanzonetta** *starts to trudge back to the cellar.*

Campanetti   Oh, Sanzonetta, I nearly forgot: I have news that may interest you.

Sanzonetta *stops.*

Campanetti   Do you remember – before your . . . condition set in – the weekend we spent in Milan?

Sanzonetta   Yes?

Campanetti   Do you remember the young man you strolled with in the garden?

Sanzonetta   Salvatore?

Campanetti   Salvatore Avaricci. You took a shine to him, if I recall?

Sanzonetta *looks down, embarrassed.*

Campanetti   Come now, admit it. You talked about him all the journey home.

Sanzonetta   I admit he was a dashing young man.

Campanetti   But he'd have nothing to do with the likes of you; isn't that what you said?

Sanzonetta   He's the heir to the Avaricci fortune . . .

Campanetti   Indeed. Well – I forgot to tell you, but I chanced to run into him recently.

Pause.

He remembered you, my sister.

Sanzonetta   He did?

Campanetti   In great detail.

Sanzonetta   Well – but – what did he say? About me?

Campanetti   He said a great deal. But to cut a long story short . . . we are to be married next spring!

Pause.

So you see: you should never judge a book by its cover. Are you happy for me?**Sanzonetta**   Of course . . .

Campanetti   Sanzonetta – look at me?

She holds her sister's face and stares at her.

Goodness, is that the time? You'd best get off to the cellar.

Campanetti *exits.* **Sanzonetta** *trudges off to the cellar.*

*

Gant   At that moment, for all her potential riches, Sanzonetta felt quite the poorest girl in the world.

The next day Campanetti set off on her trip across the water, leaving Sanzonetta alone once more. This was her sister's great error; for that week, their home received an unexpected visitor . . .

Sanzonetta *is in the cellar, dispensing pearls. A knocking from above.*

Avaricci   Hello?!

Sanzonetta *sits up, panicked.*

Sanzonetta   My goodness; who is that?!

Avaricci   Hello?!

Sanzonetta   Hello?!

Avaricci   Hello?! Where are you?!

Sanzonetta   Where is that lazy maid of ours? Drunk again, I suppose!

Avaricci   Where are you?!

Sanzonetta   I'm down here!

Avaricci   Down where?!

Sanzonetta   I shall come to you!

Avaricci   And I shall come to you!

Sanzonetta *puts on her veil and leaves the cellar.* **Avaricci** *descends the staircase. They call to each other as they draw nearer: 'Hello?!', 'Hello?!'*

Avaricci *enters at the same time as* **Sanzonetta**.

Avaricci   Campanetti!

Sanzonetta   Signor Avaricci!

Avaricci   Campanetti?

Sanzonetta   No I – I'm afraid Campanetti is in England. She is not due back until tomorrow.

Pause.

Avaricci   You do not fool me, my love. Take down that veil and let me see your beautiful face.

Sanzonetta   I am not Campanetti.

Avaricci   This is Campanetti's home, is it not?

Sanzonetta   Yes, Signor.

Avaricci   And you are no maid; for she is vomiting by the ponds. So who else lives here?

Sanzonetta   I am her sister. Sanzonetta.

Pause.

Avaricci   Campanetti – God will punish you for such wickedness!

Sanzonetta   I am who I say, Signor.

Avaricci   My dearest – you should not confuse my longings with my humour. There is a place for perversity and this is not it.

Sanzonetta   Is it so hard to believe that I am Sanzonetta?

Pause.

Avaricci   Show me your face.

Sanzonetta   I would rather not, Signor.

Avaricci *unsheaths his sword.*

Avaricci   I'm afraid I must insist.

Sanzonetta   Do not ask this of me, please.

Avaricci   This is the home of my betrothed. The door stands open. I trust you see my point.

Sanzonetta   But I am – ugly, Signor.

Avaricci   You will be more so if you do not comply this instant.

Pause.

Sanzonetta   Promise me that you will say nothing hurtful.

Avaricci   You have my word.

Sanzonetta *lowers her cowl.*

Avaricci   Dear Christ in Heaven! Your face! Your hideous, appalling face!

Sanzonetta   You promised me!

Avaricci   Why do you walk the Earth, foul fiend?! What terrible purpose have you here?! Be merciful, Sanzonetta; return to whence you came!

Sanzonetta   Your compassion overwhelms me, Signor Avaricci.

Avaricci   You have my every compassion, Sanzonetta, but you do not belong here. I would not have had you die, but die you did. Why is your spirit not at rest?!

Pause.

Sanzonetta   I am not dead, Signor.

Avaricci   No, Sanzonetta, you are – you must accept it, if you are ever to find peace!

Sanzonetta   Signor Avaricci, I assure you – I have a bad complexion, but I am not dead. Here, touch me –

Avaricci   No, get back!

Sanzonetta   Why do you think that I am dead?

Pause. She extends her hand

Touch me.

Slowly, timidly, he reaches out and touches her.

There. Am I not flesh and blood?

Pause.

Avaricci   Sanzonetta?

Pause.

But – Campanetti told me you were dead!

Sanzonetta   Campanetti?

Avaricci   Yes – I met her at a drinking contest in Bavaria. She told me you had died in Brittany, from a surfeit of eels. You mean this was a lie?

Pause. He stands.

I fear I have made a fool of myself, Signora. How can you ever forgive me?

Sanzonetta   It is not you I will need to forgive, Signor Avaricci. I suppose she also told you about the Campanetti Pearl Company?

Avaricci   Yes, in that it's a company she grew *herself* from *nothing* with *no help from anyone* and that she *personally* scours the planet for the finest pearls available, which is the reason she charges *an extra twenty per cent* over and above the asking price and that once we are married she intends to *sell* the company and use the profits to *leave this dump* and live the rest of her life in *luxury* with me in my palace in *Monaco*.

Pause.

Why?

Pause.

Sanzonetta   I think we should talk.

*

Gant   And talk, ladies and gentlemen, they did . . .

Signor Avaricci discovered the truth about his bride-to-be, and Sanzonetta showed him the true source of the so-called Campanetti pearls.

In silhouette, **Avaricci** *vomits.*

Gant   Avaricci knew then that his marriage to Campanetti was not to be. But, just as one Tutti sister was taking leave of his heart, another was stealing in . . .

*

Avaricci *and* **Sanzonetta** *return from their talk.*

Avaricci   No, he said that there was no place in the Catholic Church for the sexual molestation of children.

Sanzonetta   Did he?

Avaricci   Yes, so they're building one.

Pause.

Sanzonetta   My goodness, it has fallen dark . . .

Avaricci   Goodness, yes; so it has . . .

Sanzonetta   When did that happen?

Avaricci   I have no idea.

Pause.

Sanzonetta   Well . . .

Pause.

Avaricci   Of course you know what this means?

Sanzonetta   What?

Avaricci   The sun has crept away so as not to disturb us. It knows it has outstayed its welcome.

Sanzonetta   It is well-mannered.

Avaricci   And perceptive too.

Pause.

Avaricci   Sanzonetta – take down your veil.

Sanzonetta   Please, Signor, we have had such a pleasant afternoon. Let us not spoil it now.

Avaricci   Sanzonetta, if I have responded violently, it was to your face, not your soul.

Sanzonetta   Call me vain, but that is little comfort.

Avaricci   You must understand; despite my inordinate wealth, I am in many ways a shallow man. I have struggled for little in my life. Your sister is just the latest in a long line of impossibly beautiful women I have courted but, in truth, I have felt little for anyone.

Pause.

Until now, that is. Until meeting you.

Sanzonetta   You could not love one as ugly as I, Signor.

Avaricci   No; but that is the point. I think fate has brought me here today. I think God has sent you to me.

Sanzonetta   To what end?

Avaricci   To make me a better man.

Pause.

Sanzonetta, I will admit – my fascination with pearls is well
known. That they were Campanetti's trade played some part
in her appeal. 'But here,' God is saying, 'Look: a woman
so ugly you would not have shat in her mouth if she were
hungry. But look closer – these deformities conceal the very
thing you find most beautiful.' You see?

He gets down on one knee, holding her hand.

Loving you will be my struggle. And with God's grace I will
overcome my shallowness and find happiness at last.

Sanzonetta   Stop, Salvatore – your words pour forth like
wine and I am giddy with it!

Avaricci   As am I. But this is good; I want us to get giddy
with it!

Sanzonetta   But you are promised to my sister.

Avaricci   She has shown you no such consideration.

Pause.

Come, Sanzonetta, let your veil fall away, and with it your
chains! Let me kiss the pearls from out your skin! Let me reap
your tender harvest!

Sanzonetta   Salvatore! You have your wish, for good or ill.
Here!

She lets the cowl fall.

I give myself to you, Salvatore; Farm me! Farm me!

They embrace.

*

Gant   The very next day, Sanzonetta gathered up her
belongings and fled with Avaricci to his residence in Monaco,
where they lived out the summer in something close to bliss.

Their combined wealth was such that Sanzonetta had no
more need to sell the fruits of her skin. She grew her pearls

slowly, in the full light of day and only for her true love, Salvatore.

Avaricci *enters, dressed for all the world like a pearly king.*

Gant   Avaricci was no less content. He had been with many beautiful women in his time but – for a man obsessed with acquisition – it had never been enough. One can never truly possess a woman whose beauty is available to all men's eyes; but Sanzonetta's beauty was known only to him. She was his and his alone.

He farmed her gently, once a week, and used the pearls to build a small church on the grounds, in which they would be married as soon as work was done.

*

Sanzonetta *lies on the bed, reading a letter.*

Avaricci   What are you reading, my love?

Sanzonetta   It is from that society journal, *Buongiorno*. They wish to report on our wedding. How should we reply?

Avaricci   I tell you how we shall reply: I shall use the letter for my ablutions and we shall post it by return.

Sanzonetta   Their intentions seem quite honourable. Can we not allow their request?

Pause.

Avaricci   If it will please you, my sweet –

She embraces him. He kisses her and accidentally gets a pearl.

Another for the pulpit.

They nuzzle lovingly.

Campanetti *suddenly appears, looking wretched and poor and wearing a cowl.*

Campanetti   Ah how sweet! The Eunuch and the Jezebel!

Sanzonetta   Campanetti!

Avaricci   What brings you here?!

Campanetti   Why, Signor Avaricci – I have come to receive my invitation to your wedding, for the mail has clearly failed me! I notice you have found a use for my sister's pearls. Congratulations – a church you smell before you see. But why stop there? Perhaps you can use her other waste products for a bridal suite!

Sanzonetta   Do not blame him, my sister. I felt it would be wrong to invite you and that you would not have come, in any case.

Campanetti   Oh, but you are wrong, my sister! You may have cheated me of my business and my standing and my self-respect but make no mistake, I will be at that wedding – but not as a guest. As the Bride!

She pulls away the cowl to reveal a huge and bulbous pimple on her forehead.

You see, my love? You see what I have grown for you?

Avaricci   It's revolting, Campanetti!

Campanetti   Yes, and how I have longed to hear those words ! All those months in the dark, caked in the fat of oxen, all to hear you say those words!

Sanzonetta   What have you done to yourself?

Campanetti   Oh, do I detect fear in your voice, my traitorous sister? Then it is well placed. For now I am all a man could desire; beautiful in face and bulbous of pimple. Can you imagine the size of the fucker in this?! Why, it will put your puny petits-pois to shame!

She approaches **Avaricci**.

Campanetti   It is all for you, my love. And though my skin has grown taut as the breeches of a priest at choir practice, I have resisted all temptation to set it free. I offer it to you now, as a symbol of my devotion. Will you receive my pearl, Salvatore?

Avaricci (*tempted*)   Campanetti, I – cannot.

Campanetti   You must. You must or I shall let it grow till it impinges on my brain!

Sanzonetta   No, my sister, it will kill you!

Campanetti   If I am denied this moment, I will welcome death!

Pause.

Sanzonetta   Receive her pearl, my love.

Avaricci   Sanzonetta – are you sure?

Sanzonetta   I trust you, my darling.

Campanetti   Touching, is it not? How little she knows of the ways of men!

Sanzonetta   Perhaps. But I know the ways of mine.

Campanetti   We shall see. Once he has my pearl in his hands, we shall see how much he differs.

Pause.

Sanzonetta   Receive her pearl, Salvatore.

Pause. **Avaricci** *goes to* **Campanetti**.

Avaricci   I do this for you, my love.

Campanetti   I almost feel sorry for her.

Avaricci   Silence, woman. Deliver up your pearl.

Campanetti *uses her fists to squeeze and squeeze the huge pimple on her forehead, groaning with the effort as her sister did before her.*

Suddenly, it explodes, showering **Avaricci** *with pus. He staggers back in disgust.*

Avaricci   Achh!

Campanetti   No! No! Where is my pearl?! Where is my beautiful pearl?!

Avaricci   Get out of my palace! Get out and never return!

Campanetti   No, but it must be here! It's in here somewhere, my love, I promise you!

She searches frantically in her forehead.

Sanzonetta   There is no pearl, Campanetti, only cheese!

Avaricci   Take her from my sight, my love, take her!

Campanetti   No, please, my sweet, it is here, I tell you!

Sanzonetta   No, Campanetti – we are sisters, but this trait we do not share. Come –

Campanetti   No, wait, here – here!

She holds up a handful of jelly.

It is here, within this jelly, see – see, my love!

She searches within the jelly: nothing.

Where can it umbrella?

They look at her, puzzled.

It flog me spaghetti . . . Bubble ark abalone!

Sanzonetta   Why does she speak so strangely?

Campanetti   I cannot teat the pump garden!

Avaricci   Wait – look: this is no mere jelly; this is your brain!

Pause.

Sanzonetta   Oh no – Campanetti!

She looks at them confused.

Campanetti   The kissy summer sunshore!

Then drops down dead.

Sanzonetta and **Avaricci** *stare down at her corpse.*

*

Gant   That is a sad tale indeed, Signora; but I hope you did not blame yourself –

Sanzonetta   No, Signor Gant, I did not.

Gant   Then that is good; nor should you have. I take it, then, that the marriage did not occur?

Sanzonetta   Oh no, Signor Gant, it occurred. The marriage went ahead as planned.

Pause.

Gant   I'm not sure I understand, Signora. You said you had been much stolen from . . .

Sanzonetta   Wait, Signor Gant – my story is not ended yet.

I did marry Signor Avaricci and all was well at first. We continued our lives as happily as ever; I can recall no great disagreements, no noticeable dimming of our passion. And yet, one spring morning, I woke alone . . .

A letter lay on Salvatore's pillow . . .

She hands the letter to **Gant**.

Gant (*reads*)   'My darling Sanzonetta . . .
   'I told you once that I was a shallow man. It seems, to my shame, that this is no less true today. I can do you no more good than to state this very plainly: I have left you for an oyster named Martine.'

Pause.

'Believe me when I say you have played no part in my discontent. The restless heart is mine and mine alone.
                              'Forever yours, Salvatore Avaricci.'

Pause.

Sanzonetta   I sense, Signor Gant, that you understand what it is to lose in love, so I will not bore you with the details of my grief. But I made it then my mission to confront him and his oyster mistress.

It was a long and tiresome search, spanning much of Europe. I finally tracked them down to a diplomatic function in Vienna. I hired the most lavish dress I could and bribed the doorman fifteen pearls to let me in.

I moved through the waltzing couples as one moves through a dream. They parted before me with an almost magical precision. Finally, at the heart of the throng, I saw them . . .

Avaricci *is dancing with* **Martine** *the oyster.*

Sanzonetta   He danced with her as he once did with me. Looked at her as he once looked at me. I had played this moment in my mind so many times – how I would rage at him, show him my raw sorrow, shame him into wanting me once more.

Yet now the moment had arrived, I could but stand there. And strangely, I felt something close to tenderness. I remember thinking, here is another way in which I differ from my sister.

I let the dancers swallow me up once more, and drifted to the sidelines till the waltz came to an end.

Pause.

Gant   You did not even speak to him?

Sanzonetta   I spied him alone on the balcony later and we exchanged niceties, as if nothing so unusual had occurred.

Gant   You did not touch on his betrayal at all?

Sanzonetta   I simply asked him why– why he had left me and the bliss we had had in our grasp? What this Oyster had that I did not?

Pause.

Gant   And how did he reply?

Pause.

Sanzonetta   Mystery.

Pause.

He said she had . . . mystery.

And, with this, **Sanzonetta** *takes her leave . . .*

*

Gant   Mystery, yes . . . of course; who among us can deny
its allure? We devour it second only to food and drink.

Yet there are those who would seek to deny it. These are the
dull fellows who come to me and say, 'But Gant – you cannot
expect us to believe such a preposterous story! Surely,' they
say, 'you should devote yourself to the truth of life?'

I answer in two ways. Firstly, that I simply recount the tale as
'twere told to me. Secondly, that – whilst I have no way of
knowing what is false in Sanzonetta's story – this much I do
know; that life is not merely the space between sleeping – and
that the truth of life lies least of all in the facts.

Ladies and gentleman, you have now completed the first
course in this evening's menu. Accordingly, I shall allow you
a brief moment to digest it. I pray you will return refreshed,
your palates clean and ready for my next feat of loneliness
which I can guarantee you – in the least financial sense of
the word – will be yet more amazing still . . .

Exit.

Act Two

Gant *enters.*

Gant   I am forbidden to tell you in what way I was connected to Mr Edgar Thomas Dawn, but connected we were; and he was thus within his rights to approach me as I relaxed at the Gentleman's Club in the Rangoon Grand . . .

*

Edgar *approaches* **Gant** *at his table.*

Edgar   Sir, will you excuse me, but I must ask your assistance: and if you will shake my hand, you will understand why you must lend it, if you can.

Gant *shakes his hand. Obviously something happens.*

Gant   Gant, Edward Gant. Of the 93rd Highlanders, the Seven Oaks Order and Midget Opera T.C., at your service.

Edgar   Thank you, Brother Gant. My name is Edgar . . . Edgar Thomas . . . Dawn . . .

He sways woozily.

Gant   You seem unsteady, Brother Edgar. Here – sit down.

Edgar *nods his thanks as* **Gant** *helps him into the chair.*

Gant   Will you take your chances with the water?

Edgar   If you will grant my wish, I'll have no need of it, Brother. Nor of bread, nor sunshine, nor any of the hateful staples of existence.

Pause.

Gant   What is it you would have of me, Brother Edgar, that would render you so . . . independent?

Edgar   I would have you kill me.

Pause.

Gant   Come now, Brother. I cannot think your life is so bad.

Edgar   Can you not?

Gant   The gift you ask is grave indeed. I cannot grant it on a whim.

Edgar   No.

Pause.

No, of course not, Brother. And you must excuse my insolence. Think it only the actions of a desperate man, and remember me kindly.

He is about to go when **Gant** *stands.*

Gant   Brother Edgar.

Edgar *stops.*

Gant   I have seen death, Sir, and it is no friend of mine. But nor is it a foe. It is a tool, borrowed from God, that we use to engineer the world. Its use can be for good or ill. Perhaps if you tell me the source of your woes, I can better judge its application.

Pause.

Edgar   The source of my woes? Yes, I can tell you that and better; I can give it a name.

Louisa von Kettelmein-Kurstein Frond.

Louisa *appears, laying down a picnic blanket.*

Edgar   It hardly matters how I met her; only that I did. At first I thought her but a medley of my past loves – the smile of one, the locks of another, the careless shrug of another still . . . But it soon came clear my Louisa was no pale reminder of them; but rather they who had served to point the way to her.

Pause.

She was my fate, Brother Gant, come down in female form. I had no choice but to love her . . .

*

A field. **Louisa** *is eating as* **Edgar** *returns.*

Louisa   Jammy ring?

Edgar   No, no, I used a dockleaf.

Louisa   No, I mean would you care for a jammy ring? Papa made them this morning.

Edgar   Really? Well; what a peculiar name.

He watches her lovingly.

How funny you are.

Louisa   In what respect?

Edgar   Oh, I don't know. With your little nose and your . . . jammy, jammy ring.

Louisa   Am I your great, great love?

Edgar   It would appear that you are.

Pause.

Louisa   I am bereft of undergarments.

Pause.

Edgar   How funny you are.

Pause.

No, but I think you are . . . I think you are my great love – I know you are – which brings me quite neatly to what I was going to say and why I brought you here today, to where we first ever kissed; it seemed the right place for me to ask you this – thing I'm going to ask you –

Louisa *lifts out another cake.*

Edgar   No, don't have another jammy ring –

Louisa   They're delicious!

Edgar   No, but – because I'm going to ask you something.

Louisa   So?

Edgar   Well, just – please, my dearest – you can have one, just – wait a moment . . .

She sits with the jammy ring hovering at her mouth.

No, can you –

Louisa   What?

Edgar   Can you actually just – Louisa, my dearest –

Louisa   It's attracting flies!

Edgar   Just one moment –

Louisa   I wish you would just say what it is then, and be done with it!

Edgar   No, but it requires –

Louisa   These damnable flies !

Edgar   I'm asking for your hand –

Pause.

Louisa   In marriage?

Edgar   In marriage, yes; my sweetheart, my darling, my sunshine and showers.

Pause.

Louisa   I have no words.

Edgar   You need only one.

Louisa   And you don't mind about my . . . ?

She looks down at herself.

Edgar   I wouldn't have them any other way.

She suddenly embraces him.

Louisa   Edgar, my love! I do, I will. Yes! My love.

Edgar   I think I have never been happier than now. And it seems all nature does agree!

Louisa   Ow!

She touches her neck.

I think I have been bitten . . .

Edgar   I see the culprit – a foul and vicious wasp. How dare you sting my sweet Louisa?!

He beats it to death.

There. He has paid full penalty for his crime.

But **Louisa** *is going into shock . . .*

Edgar   'Tis only a wasp's sting, my sweet . . .

Louisa   I feel strange . . .

Edgar   Have you not been stung before?

Pause.

Louisa?

Louisa   Something is happening to me . . .

Edgar   What?

She begins to shake uncontrollably.

Louisa! What is wrong with you?!

Louisa   I don't know – the world is turning black –

Edgar   What do you mean?

Louisa   I fear I am . . . slipping away – Edgar . . .

Edgar   No, don't be absurd – !

Louisa   I'm losing you, my love –

Edgar   But it's only a wasp sting – Louisa . . . !

Louisa   Hush now, hush – There is no better day to die.

Edgar   No, Louisa, listen; this cannot be! It was only a wasp, you cannot die – I forbid you to die, Louisa, I FORBID IT!

He looks around for help, distraught.

Louisa   Know that I would have married you, Edgar. That there is another world where I did, and where we still wake up together – only now the birdsong is joined with the laughter of our children. It is there I go to be with you now . . .

Edgar   Then I will follow!

She grabs him, urgently.

Louisa   No! No, you must promise me – you must live your life in joy, you must do that for me!

Edgar   No – Louisa –

Louisa   It is a sin, Edgar – you must not sin for me. If you join me it must be God's will alone. Promise me, Edgar, if you love me. Promise me.

Pause.

Edgar   I promise.

Louisa   You can – have those – jammy rings . . .

And with this, she dies.

*

Edgar   Need I tell you, Brother Gant, that God made an enemy that day?

It seemed I was no longer flesh and bone and sinew but a creature carved of pain alone.

For years I raged from place to place, fighting, drinking and trying to womanise. I became hopelessly addicted to opium and even sank so low as to canvas for Gladstone. I knew things had to change.

Despite the Liberal Government, I made the decision to go on with life. I destroyed every letter sent me by Louisa, every rendering of her. Anything I could find that in any way conjured her, I loaded on a pyre and burned from out my sight.

But still I could not free myself from the quicksands of my grief. One image of her remained to haunt me, outwit my grasp, unburnable.

He taps his forehead.

Here, my Brother, here it was stored; within my mind's imagining. Playing like a diorama in my skull.

I thought myself beyond hope; until that chance encounter in an opium den in Hastings . . .

*

A **Man** *lies on a mattress, out of his head on opium.*

Man   That is a sad tale, my friend, and I can offer no solution –

Edgar   You misunderstand me, Sir, I was not –

Man   Hold on, you didn't let me finish. I can offer no solution but one. Tell me: are you a wealthy man?

Edgar   Once I was of reasonable means, but no longer.

Man   A pity.

Edgar   Why a pity? There are no riches on this earth enough to buy peace for my soul.

Man   Wrong, Sir. The rich can buy anything; a round trip to Nepal, for example.

Edgar   I do not need a holiday, Sir.

Man   It would be far from that. This would require a treacherous journey into the mountain ranges, the most inhospitable terrain known to man.

Edgar   And why would I choose to holiday there?

Man   You would not. Instead, you would seek out Ranjeev the Uncomplicated, an ancient fakir who has made his home there.

Edgar   And why would I holiday with him?

Pause. The **Man** *is still.* **Edgar** *shakes him.*

Man   Eh?

Edgar   Why would I holiday with Ranjeev the Uncomplicated?

Man   You would not. But rumour has it he can lift the torment from men's minds as cleanly as you would lift a bullet from out a leg.

Edgar   You mean – he could rid me of this last image of Louisa?

Man   It is only rumour, my friend. But I don't see why not.

Pause.

Edgar   He is a fakir, you say?

Man   An old fakir, yes.

Edgar   An old Indian fakir.

They begin to laugh.

Man   A wizened old fakir!

The laughter grows uncontrollable.

Edgar   Here – I hope the 'fakir' is not a 'faker' –

They lose themselves in hysterics.

Man   I wish you well, my friend!

The laughter subsides. Pause.

Have you got anything to eat?

*

Gant   Decency prohibits me from telling you how this tortured soul went about raising the money for his expedition to Nepal. Let us just say that, after two years in Plymouth, he was of sufficient means to set sail for the East.

By the time Edgar neared the summit of the range, he was alone; his sherpas having either died, fled or simply gone in the huff with him. A terrible snowstorm blew up and Edgar found himself exhausted and consumed. He lay there, near the roof of the world, and drifted into unconsciousness . . .

*

Edgar *wakes in a cave.*

Edgar   Where am I? What is this place? Hello?!

Backstage, the other players provide the echo to his words.

No reply but my own . . . Perhaps I have died. Yes: perhaps I have died and gone to Heaven!

But if this is Heaven, where is my sweet Louisa's welcome? Where be the cherubs and their tender ministrations? And why is my mouth as dry as a suffragette's chuff?

Perhaps this is not Heaven, but the other place. Have I been so wretched in my grief? Has God turned his back on one so taken with his own misfortune? Forgive me, gentle one, I implore you! Be merciful in death to one so robbed in life! I beseech you, Lord! I beseech you!

He collapses in tears. **Ranjeev** *enters.*

Ranjeev   Excuse me, Sir, but I was wondering if you would mind beseeching your God a little quieter, as the sound does tend to travel.

Edgar   Who are you?

Ranjeev   I am the one you seek.

Edgar   You are Ranjeev the Uncomplicated?

Ranjeev   In a word: yes.

Edgar   Then this is not the Promised Land?

Ranjeev   No, it's a cave.

Edgar   But nor is it Hell itself.

Pause.

Ranjeev   It's a cave.

Edgar   Your name is well earned.

Ranjeev *nods his thanks.*

Edgar *looks back out of the cave entrance.*

Ranjeev   It is true to say you came close to death. Moments more and the mountain would have claimed you.

Edgar   Yes, I remember feeling wretchedly cold . . . and sitting down for a rest and then . . . I must've fainted, like a woman. How dreadfully embarrassing.

Ranjeev   No, no, Sahib – This mountain is known for its treacherous cold. This is why the natives know it as Sangavi-al-jaheer.

Edgar   Which means?

Ranjeev   Mountain of treacherous cold.

Edgar   Treacherous indeed: even thick tweed offers no protection.

Ranjeev   That is what I most admire about the English; at their most stylish when style is least required.

Edgar   Thank you, my friend. But – English or not – it would seem I owe you my thanks.

Ranjeev   Sir, please – I need no thanks for what I did.

Edgar   Allow me their expression at least.

Ranjeev   I neither need nor deserve them.

Edgar   On the contrary, you deserve a great deal more. You ventured outside, at no little risk to yourself, and dragged me to safety, did you not?

Ranjeev   Yes . . .

Edgar   Then why would you not deserve my gratitude?

Ranjeev   Because your ear broke off.

He shows **Edgar** *the ear.*

*

Gant   Later – when the screaming had ceased – Edgar told the mystic of his plight. Ranjeev the Uncomplicated sat silent and serene throughout the recounting and pondered his answer long and hard . . .

*

A long, hard pause. Finally, **Ranjeev** *speaks.*

Ranjeev   It is true what they say. I can do this thing you ask.

Pause.

Edgar   Pardon?

Ranjeev   IT IS TRUE WHAT THEY SAY. I CAN DO THIS THING YOU ASK.

Edgar   Oh, right, good.

Ranjeev   And so do all respond at first. But there are –

Edgar *cups his non-existent ear.*

Ranjeev   BUT THERE ARE DANGERS HERE.

Edgar *still can't hear. He turns so that his existing ear is towards* **Ranjeev**.

Ranjeev   THERE ARE – there are dangers here.

Edgar   I am content with that. All that matters is I am freed of this torment; the means are unimportant.

Ranjeev   With respect, Sahib: there is worse in life than death.

Edgar   Than my death, yes. Than hers – than my beloved Louisa's death – no, my friend: there was no worse, not in my life. Nor will there ever be.

Pause.

Ranjeev   Very well.

He rises.

It will require me exposing the very essence of your being. Touching the very core of the tortured soul within you.

Edgar   And how will this come about? Through meditation, song and deep massage?

Ranjeev *opens a box full of horrendous trepanation items.*

Ranjeev   No. By drilling a hole in your head.

Pause. **Edgar** *stares at the gruesome instruments.*

Edgar   I see. So it is to be done with trepanation.

Ranjeev   Oh yes; with *extreme* trepanation.

Edgar   *Extreme* trepanation?

Ranjeev   It cannot be done lightly.

Edgar   No, I suppose not.

Pause.

Purely as a matter of interest – could you refresh me as to what exactly this procedure involves?

Ranjeev   The spike takes purchase of the skull, anchoring the cutting tool as it shears a perfect circle from its hard, bony plate. The disc is removed, laying bare the throbbing brain. Then I will introduce a device that will apply pressure to the brain whilst also acting to close the wound.

Pause.

Edgar   Righty-ho . . .

Ranjeev   You will no longer be plagued by the image of your loss –

Edgar   Well, that's the main thing . . .

Ranjeev   Listen carefully, Sahib. The image of your beloved will be gone, but not the memory of what occurred. You will know that you loved and that you lost. But your memories will be like empty rooms.

Edgar   The emptier the better.

Ranjeev   There is one thing further: once this device is in place, it can never be removed. The moment it is removed, the image of your beloved will return and blood will flood your head, bringing instant death. Do you understand, Sahib? You cannot remove it, even for a moment.

Edgar   I understand.

Ranjeev   Not even if it gets itchy.

Edgar   Not even if it gets itchy.

Ranjeev   It does get very itchy.

Edgar   Listen – I was in the Camel Corps. There's nothing you can tell me about itching.

Pause.

Your well-meaning words are noted, my friend, and well taken 'n all. I came here to find peace, by hook or by crook. You have my blessing to proceed.

Ranjeev   As you wish.

Standing behind **Edgar**, **Ranjeev** *assembles the diabolical trepanatory tool.*

Ranjeev   Will you be going on holiday this year?

Edgar   I shouldn't think so. Spent all my money coming here.

Ranjeev   I know; it's so expensive, is it not?

Edgar   It's not so much the travelling as paying the guides not to kill you.

Ranjeev   It's terrible. Now, I'm just going to take a little off the top, nothing off the back.

Edgar   Proceed.

Alarmingly, **Ranjeev** *is consulting an instruction manual.*

He gently taps the spike, trying to penetrate **Edgar**'s *skull.* **Edgar** *does his best to cope.*

Edgar   Goodness. What a very strange sensation.

Pause.

So at the moment you're attempting to penetrate my skull, are you?

Ranjeev   That is correct, Sir.

Edgar   Right.

Ranjeev   Try not to nod, Sahib.

Edgar   Right, of course.

Pause. **Ranjeev** *looks perplexed. It isn't working and the manual makes no sense.*

Edgar   It's typical, isn't it? All these years of torment I've suffered and yet, now, sitting here, it doesn't seem so very bad. I think it might be the mountain air.

Pause.

Not that I'm saying we shouldn't proceed or anything. Just, it would be funny, wouldn't it, if I was sitting here having my skull opened when all I really needed was a holiday! It'd be just like the thing.

Ranjeev *stops. The manual requires another piece of kit to be used. He sees the instrument in the trepanation box.*

Ranjeev   There we are . . .

Edgar *stands.*

Edgar   Oh, well – that wasn't so bad, was it? Bit of sweat on the old palms but apart from that . . . Almost relaxing in its way.

Ranjeev   I have done nothing, Sahib.

Edgar   You're too modest, my friend. I can tell you are greatly skilled.

Ranjeev   No, I really have done nothing, Sir. The spike is not yet in.

Pause.

Edgar   Not even a bit?

Ranjeev *sits him back down.*

Edgar   But it was bloody agony!

Ranjeev   It will be easier now. Hold your nerve, Sahib.

Edgar   Look – I'm holding my nerve but – it is clean, isn't it? This spike thing?

Ranjeev   Perfectly. Hold still.

He screws down the cutting tool.

Edgar   Oh dear! That was − a tad painful.

Pause.

You're sure that it's clean, are you?

Ranjeev   Are you suggesting that we Indians are dirty, Sahib?

Edgar   No, not at all, I just −

Another grind on the implement.

Oh, Ma*ma*!

Ranjeev   I know that is what you English think. That we are no cleaner than the dogs you accuse us of eating.

Edgar   No, you misunderstand me −

Ranjeev   You think that we do our business in the street, like animals.

Edgar   I can assure you, Ranjeev, I meant no −

And one more for luck.

Ranjeev   We are in, Sahib!

Edgar   Oh − ! Good show.

Ranjeev   Now − this is where it gets messy . . .

*

Gant   Ladies and gentlemen − we shall spare both you and the laundryman the gory spectacle that followed.

Suffice it to say that it was all over within twelve hours . . .

*

Ranjeev *is soaked with blood.*

Edgar *sits, harrowed, with his hand on his head.*

Ranjeev *holds a long cork.*

Ranjeev   Now, Sahib, the hole has been cut and the brain is exposed. Can you still recall the face of your beloved?

Edgar   The what?

Ranjeev   The face of the woman that you loved.

Edgar   Oh, Louisa. Yes. Yes, I can.

Ranjeev   Then savour it, Sahib. It is for the last time.

Edgar   Goodbye, my love, until God brings us together once more.

Ranjeev   Now – when I tell you – remove your hand and I will push in the cork, thereby ridding you of your pain.

Pause.

Now, Sahib – remove your hand!

He does so, and – with some effort – **Ranjeev** *pushes the cork into* **Edgar***'s head.*

Ranjeev   It is in, Sahib. The cork is in!

Edgar   Thank the Lord!

Ranjeev   Give me your hand –

He places **Edgar***'s hand on top of the cork.*

Ranjeev   Now you must maintain this pressure on the cork. The blood in your skull will solidify around it, locking it to your brain.

Edgar   How long will it take?

Ranjeev   A month, to be safe.

Edgar   A month?! I can't walk around like this for a month!

Ranjeev   You must, Sir. If the cork comes loose, you will die instantaneously!

Edgar   Then I must endure the indignity. For I swore to my Louisa that I would never –

Pause.

Wait! What is this?! I still see her face!

Pause.

Ranjeev! I still see my Louisa's face! Only now – 'tis more vivid than ever!

Pause.

No! I see her as she died – her face as she died! My poor Louisa, no! I can think of nothing else! Something has gone wrong, Ranjeev! The surgery has failed!

Ranjeev   Oh.

Pause.

Well – I tried.

Edgar   What do you mean, you tried?! No – Louisa! She haunts me worse than ever! What have you done to me, you swine?!

Ranjeev   Look – I tried, it didn't work out; what do you want me to say?

Edgar   But – I thought you had done this before!?

Ranjeev   Yes, but not on a man!

Edgar   Not on a man?

Ranjeev   No, on one of those, what do you call them – a goat.

Edgar   A goat?!

Ranjeev   Goats have feeling too, you know.

Pause.

Well, not this one; not any more.

Edgar   You have not performed it on yourself?

Ranjeev   You think I am insane?!

Edgar   But what am I to do?! The image of her dying is fixed behind my eyes as if I lost her only yesterday!

Ranjeev   You are so impatient, you English. You think you take what you want, exactly when you want it. In your impatience to escape the pain of loss, you have made it more so. You have brought this on yourself.

Edgar   How dare you blame me for your incompetence?! Why, I ought to strangle you where you stand!

Ranjeev   You would need both hands for that, Sahib.

Edgar   You fiend!

Ranjeev   I am a mild man, Sahib, but I will not be insulted in my own cave.

He bustles **Edgar** *out.*

Edgar   You can't send me out in this condition!

Ranjeev   Watch me.

He bundles him out.

Edgar   God will punish you for this, Ranjeev.

Ranjeev   My God can take your God any day!

Edgar   No, he can't!

Ranjeev   There are two ways down the mountain, Sahib. A quick way and a slow way. I would advise you take the slow way.

Pause.

And don't come back!

*

Back in Rangoon . . .

Edgar   So now you understand why I ask you for a favour so grave, Brother Gant.

I have lived this last year in the most debilitating torment. I sleep only minutes at a time. Even opium offers only momentary relief.

I would have removed this infernal cork long ago were it not for my promise to Louisa. This is why it must be the work of another to deliver me unto God.

What say you, Brother? Will you do what I ask?

A long pause, then **Gant** *rises.*

Gant   Ladies and gentlemen – I have decided to curtail this story for reasons that will later be revealed.

Gant *walks off, leaving* **Edgar** (**Jack Dearlove**) *bewildered on stage. Pause.*

Jack *is about to leave the stage, when* **Gant** *returns.*

Gant   I have decided also to forego our usual interval. We shall continue with the show momentarily.

He leaves again, taking **Jack** *with him.*

There is a long moment of silence, while the stage stands empty . . .

Eventually, the player, **Nicholas Ludd**, *enters.*

Ludd   Ladies and gentlemen – while my fellow-actors prepare the stage for our next story, I should like to meanwhile occupy you with some poems of my own devising. The first is entitled 'The Night Watchman'.

Pause.

> All night,
> He watches
> The night.
> The night
> Watchman
>
> The day
> He does not watch,
> He's not
> The day
> Watchman
>
> One day
> He might watch

The day
But not
Tonight.

Tonight
He watches
The night,
The night
Watchman.

Pause.

Thank you.

He looks behind to see if they are ready yet. They are not.

My next poem is entitled, 'What Need Have I of Whimsy?'

Pause.

What need have I of whimsy?
Give me potatoes instead
My child can live without whimsy
Without 'taters, she will be dead.

What need have I of your whimsy?
Repeal the Corn Laws instead
My family can live without whimsy
The Corn Laws will see us all dead

Pause.

Give me not your whimsy
Give me 'taters and Corn Laws –

No –

Pause.

Give me not your whimsy
Give me 'taters and – have the Corn Laws, um –

He stops, obviously having dried.

. . –

. . *use. And then, the sound of thunder: smoke billows onto the stage.*

. . *cloak drifts on. It is* **Gant**.

Gant   Nicholas Ludd!

Ludd   Who are you?

Gant   I am the Phantom of the Dry! I appear to thespians whose lines have escaped them; I live a whole lifetime in those yawning seconds of helplessness and pass, like a butterfly, when they end!

Ludd   Have you come to me with my lines, Phantom?

Gant   I have not. I bring instead a lesson.

Ludd   What good is a lesson to me now, when the audience is hanging on my words?

Gant   The only thing this audience will be hanging is you, my friend, for your crimes against poetry!

Pause.

Ludd   I think they would rather my poems than your whimsy. Wouldn't you, ladies and gentlemen?

He addresses this to the audience, who will more than likely ignore him.

Gant   An overwhelming response. Nonetheless, let me return to the lesson –

Pause.

I hear your thoughts, thespian! You stand here at a loss and think yourself the loneliest soul in the world, am I correct?

Ludd   No.

Pause.

Gant   I think so!

Ludd   No, actually.

Gant   Yes, and you should be ashamed! Take my hand and I shall put your selfish thoughts to rest!

Ludd *takes his hand. There is a flash, and they are transported.*

Ludd   My goodness! Where have you taken me, terrible Phantom of the Dry?!

Gant   To the land of the small hours, where the lonely wander endlessly!

Ludd   Wait – where are you going?

Gant   I told you – I live only the few yawning seconds of your helplessness; I have no intention of spending them with you.

Pause.

I will return when you have learnt the error of your ways; or remembered the next line of your poem – whichever comes first.

He exits, dramatically.

Ludd   What a fat and *whimsical* fool! His strategy is doomed to failure; for if I were not the loneliest creature on earth when he plucked me up, I most surely am now!

Pause.

Give me not your whimsy . . .
Give me corn and –

No, that's not it . . .

*A full-size **Bear** appears in the background.*

Bear One   Excuse me, Sir?

Ludd *turns.*

Ludd   Good Lord! A full-grown bear!

Bear One   Please, kind Sir, I mean you no harm. I am merely a child's plaything, abandoned and astray.

Ludd   What do you want of me?

Bear One   Only a few pennies, Sir – a few pennies for an imaginary cup of tea. Can you spare it?

Ludd   Imaginary, did you say?

Bear One   Yes, Sir, an imaginary cup of tea, just to keep ⌐ on such a night. Can you spare it, Sir?

Ludd   I'm afraid I have no money.

Bear One   None, Sir?

Ludd   None. In fact, I am not even here.

Bear One   Where are you, Sir?

Ludd   I'm on stage in Plymouth. I've just dried.

Bear One   Dried, Sir ?

Ludd   Forgotten my lines.

Bear One   Oh, I see. That must be lonely, right enough. That must be the loneliest thing in the world.

Ludd   Exactly my point.

Bear One   So you're an actor, then?

Ludd   I try.

Bear One   And what are you currently drying in?

Ludd   An unintelligible travelling vanity project by an opium-addicted buffoon who thinks himself a visionary!

Bear One (*nods*)   Cos I'm in showbusiness myself. Nothing so grand as that, of course. I've just got a song that I sing so's to make a few pennies. I'll sing it for you, if you like. It's very nice, and all for the price of an imaginary cup of tea.

Ludd   Look, I've told you –

Bear One   Yes, Sir, you have. It's just often people say they ain't got none, when they have.

Ludd   Yes, well, this time I'm telling the truth.

Pause.

You have your answer, bear; be off with you. I am trying to recall my lines.

Bear One   Perhaps I can help you, Sir.

Pause.

And all for the price of an imaginary cup of tea.

Ludd   If you ask me that again, Bear − !

Bear One   I'm sorry, Sir − please don't beat me. It's just that I am so very, very thirsty.

Pause.

Ludd
　Give me not your whimsy,
　Bring me Corn Laws and −

*The **Bear** is hanging around.*

Ludd   Be off with you then.

Bear One   Yes, Sir. Sorry, Sir.

*The **Bear** trudges away slowly. Pause.*

Ludd   Look − if all you want is an imaginary cup of tea, why not simply make it yourself?

Bear One   Oh no, Sir, that's not how it works. I can't make myself one, no. There'd be no point in that at all.

Ludd   Why not?

Bear One   Because it's not the tea, Sir, it's the whole thing − having it made for you, having someone hold it to your mouth, pour it in . . . Oh, it's grand, Sir.

Ludd   I'm sure there must be someone in this lonely land who will do this for you.

Bear One   There is a filthy old tramp, Sir, who will do imaginary things for money. All the abandoned playthings go to him.

Ludd   Would he not consider waiving his fee?

Bear One   He sometimes forgoes the money, Sir. But there is always a fee.

*The **Bear** hides its face in shame.*

Ludd   Good God! What kind of a hell have you brought me to, cruel Phantom of the Dry?!

Pause.

But where is your owner, Bear? I take it you had one once?

Bear One   Oh, yes, Sir. Indeed. And he was good to me, Sir, good as gold. What happened – it wasn't his fault, not really. He fell in with a bad lot, is all, and that's easily done, let me tell you.

Ludd   What is it that happened?

Pause.

Bear One   I'd rather not go into it, Sir, if it's all the same to you.

Ludd   Why not?

Bear One   It just upsets me, is all. I'd really rather not.

Pause.

Ludd   I tell you what: if you recount what happened . . . I'll make you some imaginary tea.

Pause.

Bear One   You would do that for me? What about cake?

Ludd   Imaginary cake?

The **Bear** *nods.*

Ludd   Go on then, yes. If you will tell me what happened.

Pause.

Bear One   I was with him since he was a baby. Gorgeous, he was: golden hair in loose, silky curls. He used to worry about me dying, you know. 'What will I do when you die?' he would say. Sometimes he would say it over and over, till he brought himself to tears. To tears, Sir. And then he would hug me tight to his chest.

Pause.

But he changed, Sir. He'd always been a bright and happy soul but all of a sudden he was filled with self-loathing.

Ludd   Self-loathing?

Bear One   Oh, yes, Sir. He would hit himself, Sir.

Ludd   Hit himself?

Bear One   Yes, Sir. He would turn my face to the pillow but I could hear him, Sir, beating himself mercilessly, sometimes two or three times a day. Harrowing, it was, Sir – I mean, why would a young boy beat himself so?

Ludd   I daresay he had his reasons.

Bear One   Oh, but not only that, Sir –

Ludd   No?

Bear One   He was constantly wanking as well, Sir.

Ludd   I am growing impatient with this story, Bear!

Bear One   He fell in with some boys, Sir. Not bad boys in themselves but cruel, as boys can be. One day, they saw me on the bed and they mocked my friend; said he was a weakling, Sir, and a mummy's boy. He denied it, of course. He said I was just there by accident, but they didn't believe him. They picked me up and threw me back and forth. I could see my friend was upset and so could they, which only fired them with further mischief. 'Don't cry, Sir,' I was thinking. 'Don't let them see you care,' and he managed, Sir – he kept the tears at bay. They were almost convinced. But there was one more test to pass . . .

Pause.

'If you truly don't care about this stupid toy,' they said, 'Let us see you torture it.'

Ludd   How beastly!

Bear One   They bashed my head off the bureau and twisted my arms and punched my nose. Then they threw me to my friend. 'Punch him,' they said, and soon they were taunting and chanting and it wasn't his fault, Sir, he couldn't resist.

Pause.

He punched me. Just gently at first; but the boys all cheered, so he did it again, harder this time, and then again and then, like a fire, the laughter spread to my friend and I knew then. I knew I had lost him.

Pause.

Later on, he hugged me and wept and said he was sorry but I was never allowed back on the bed. I sat on the chair for months and then the lady put me in the cupboard.

Pause.

Ludd   That is a strangely depressing story.

Pause.

Bear One   May I have my tea and cake now?

Pause.

Ludd   Yes. Of course.

*Fuming with embarrassment, **Ludd** sets about making the imaginary tea in painstaking detail, while the **Bear** looks eagerly on.*

He cuts a slice of cake and puts it alongside the tea on an imaginary tray.

*He carries it to the **Bear** and lifts the cup to its lips. It starts to drink.*

*Another **Bear** appears at the back, watches for a moment, then approaches.*

Bear Two   Is that imaginary tea you're having?

Ludd   No, sod this – I'm not having this! This is ludicrous! GANT?!

He turns to the audience.

I'm sorry, ladies and gentlemen, but I can't go on with this. I'M NOT GOING ON WITH THIS, GANT, DO YOU HEAR ME?!

Bear Two (*whispers*)   What are you doing, Ludd?!

Ludd   I'm stopping the show, Jasper – that's all right, isn't it? To just stop the show when you feel like it?!

Bear Two (*whispers*)   Of course it's not all right!

Ludd   Well it's all right for Gant – it's all right for him, isn't it? So why's it not all right for me?! COME ON, GANT! SHOW YOURSELF!

Bear Two *then attempts to manhandle him off the stage.*

Ludd   Get your hands off me, Jasper! I won't be silenced!

Bear One (**Madame Poulet**) *takes her head off and approaches the audience. She has a tiny body strapped to her chin.*

Poulet   Ladies and gentlemen – I know it doesn't look like it, but this is actually meant to happen –

Ludd   Don't tell them that! Ladies and gentlemen –

Bear Two *tackles him again, bringing him to the floor. They grapple on the stage.*

Poulet   Um – the bear and the man did then wrestle most um – wrestlingly – upon the floor –

Ludd *breaks free.* (*Note: in these sequences, the lines are of secondary importance to the realistic creation of chaos.* **Poulet** *may improvise this mock-narration at her discretion.*)

Ludd   Come on, Poulet, what's the matter?! This is what he wants, isn't it?! Give the people a show! Well, here you go, ladies and gentlemen! Nicholas Ludd's amazing feat of sanity!

Bear Two   Shut up, Ludd!

Ludd   I've had enough of it, Jasper; he's made a monkey out of me, out of all of us, for far too long!

Bear Two   He hasn't made a monkey out of me.

Ludd   Oh don't be ridiculous; look at yourself, man! Look at her! Look at this –

the little body strapped to **Madame Poulet**'s *chin.*

Do you know what this is, ladies and
    bortion! She comes on later as a

Backstreet Abortion! Now how pointless – and tasteless – and sick is that?!

Bear Two *attacks him again.* **Madame Poulet** *tries to drag them apart.*

Gant *appears on the balcony.*

Gant   Jack!

They stop and look up at him.

Let him be.

Ludd *struggles to his feet.*

Ludd   Ah, there he is! There he is, ladies and gentlemen, the great Edward Gant: prodigy, soldier, traveller, poet, but always and ever an absolute bulb! Well, I've had it, Gant, do you hear me?! I've had it with your lies and your pretentiousness! I'm leaving this flea-bitten show once and for all!

Bear Two *takes his head off: it is, of course,* **Jack Dearlove**.

Jack   I'll not have that, Ludd. I'll not have you call Mr Gant a liar!

Ludd   Oh, wake up, you old fool! He's lied to us all along! You think he's ever going to put in your stupid war story?

Jack   Next season, actually, yes.

Ludd   It's dung, Jasper, and you know it! We won't be doing your war story, any more than anything with any kind of reality at all!

Pause.

Never mind that there's writers out there trying to deal with real people and real issues! 'Yes, Nicky, but we have to Trojan Horse it,' he says. Three years later and the only horse we've had is the one with the magic cock! He's betrayed us! You've betrayed us, Gant! And those are *my* poems, and they're *good* poems, they have *meaning* – which is more than this piece of nonsense has – and you used them for a cheap joke! Well not any more! And I *know* the next lines, ladies and gentlemen:

Give me none of your whimsy,
Give me potatoes and corn,
For whimsy is made for the dying
Not for the ones being born!

He bows.

I thank you! I thank you!

Gant *claps.*

Gant   Bravo, Nicky; very good. I always knew you had it in you.

Jack   Mr Gant, should I . . . ?

He nods towards the audience.

Gant   No, no, Nicky is right. We have no secrets from them. And he's right about something else. I have betrayed you. All of you.

He sets off down to them. Pause as they consider his pronouncement.

Poulet   Does that mean I can take off my abortion?

Jack   I don't know what any of it means!

Ludd   It means I'm right, Jasper.

Jack   My name is Jack, do you understand?! Jack Jack Jack! And you've got no right to talk to Mr Gant like that, to call him a liar! Why he's the bravest, most honest man I ever met!

Ludd   And he saved your life, I know – !

Jack   He did save my life! He did, ladies and gentlemen. The Charge of the Light Brigade, it was, and I had come off my horse, and I was lying there in the mud and the blood – the blood and the mud – the mud and the blood!

He passes out.

Ludd   And that's as far as he ever gets with *that* story, ladies and gentlemen.

Madame Poulet *starts to strut and cluck like a chicken.*

Ludd   Dear God . . . !

Poulet
    Ladies and gentlemen, do not go!
    Guess what I've got down below?
    Watch, as from, between my legs,
    I drop half-a-dozen eggs!

Pause.

Does anyone happen to have a hard-boiled egg at all? In its shell, preferably.

Gant *enters.*

Gant   It's all right, Madame Poulet.

Jack *stands to attention, salutes.*

Jack   Dearlove, Sergeant, Jack, Sir!

Gant   At ease, Sergeant.

Pause.

Ladies and gentlemen; as you can see, our performance has taken an unexpected turn. You are free to leave if such candour embarrasses you.

Jack *starts to leave.*

Gant   Not you, Jack.

Jack   Sir, I must register my disapproval of this business.

Gant   Noted, Sergeant.

Jack   Thank you, Sir.

Ludd   'Thank you, Sir.' Listen to him!

Jack   You need a lesson in loyalty, Ludd, and I'm just the man to give it you!

Ludd   Ah, Jack – the thing with people like you is that you need to be led, and it doesn't matter why or by who! You're a company man, Jack!

Jack   I don't take that as an insult.

Ludd   I didn't think you would.

Poulet   You are being unfair, Mr Ludd. We all owe Mr Gant a great deal. You, for one, would be in prison for treason.

Ludd   That's a damnable lie and you will retract it!

Poulet   I will not. You attended a Royal Gala with explosives strapped to your chest; what is that if it is not treason?

Ludd   I told you – it was a corset sold me by an Irishman! But even so, what of it? Does it mean I am in his debt for ever? What is the point of saving someone only to enslave them?!

Gant   You have always been free to leave, Mr Ludd.

Ludd   You said you had a vision!

Gant   I did. And this is it.

Ludd   Exactly. This is it. This is your examination of loneliness. Nothing about the poor or the needy, the sick or the dispossessed. Just a mish-mash of preposterous stories and cheap innuendoes.

Poulet   To be fair, Mr Ludd, most of the cheap innuendoes are yours.

Ludd   That's not the point! What does it have to do with the real loneliness of real people?!

Gant   Nicholas, Nicholas – this has always been your problem; you can never see the woods for the trees.

Ludd   No, Gant – it's you that cannot see what is happening all around you. These people want to see real life as it is lived, not the opium-fuelled fantasies of an egotist! And if we do not give what they seek, they will turn away from the theatre and who will remain to play to? The rich and the idle, and that is all!

Gant (*amused*)   Don't forget the critics. Whose ranks it seems you have joined.

Ludd   How dare you!

Gant   No, you show great aptitude. You have that rare ability to misinterpret a man's aims and then hound him for not achieving them.

Jack   Genius, Sir. (*To* **Ludd**.) That's genius, that is.

Ludd   Oh, shut up, Jasper!

Jack   Don't you call me that, Ludd!

Ludd   Gant is no genius!

Jack   Tell him not to call me that, Sir!

Ludd   I'm just saying that we had a chance here; but you're still running a freak show! And we are the freaks!

Pause.

Gant   Are we done now?

Ludd   Yes, I am done. Well and truly done.

Pause.

Gant   Mr Ludd is correct. I am no genius and have never claimed to be. In fact, I doubt the word itself; it is merely the term used by the talented to account for those more talented than themselves.

Jack   Genius!

Pause.

I mean . . .

Gant   Oh, my friends, my friends. What a long road has brought us here.

Pause.

Mr Ludd makes a fair point. There is real loneliness out there and an appetite to see it reflected. But that is not what this show is about. It is not about survival, but all that is superfluous to survival: love and dreams and imagination and . . . love.

Pause. He ventures into the audience.

In a world where death is at our shoulder every hour, even the smallest act of creativity is a marvellous, courageous thing. The fact that this audience has come here tonight, to dream along with us – that is an act of courage, of hope; an amazing feat of loneliness. Do you see?

Pause.

Poulet   But why did you say you had betrayed us?

Gant   I have betrayed you because I have been dishonest. I have compromised the truth for the sake of entertainment. (*To* **Ludd**.) Not reality; the truth.

Pause.

But you are right, Mr Ludd. We cannot go on with this. There will be no more. This will be the last show.

Poulet   The last?!

Jack   With respect, Sir, have you taken leave of your senses? You cannot be swayed by this guttersnipe!

Ludd   How dare you call me guttersnipe?!

Gant   Please, gentlemen. The decision is mine alone.

Poulet   But why, Edward, why?

Pause.

Gant   Edgar Thomas Dawn: a man who felt the pain of loss so strongly that he undergoes cruel and brutal surgery.

Pause.

In our story, the operation goes wrong and he is condemned to live with the image of his loss for ever. Now what is this saying?

Jack   Never trust an Indian, Sir.

Gant   Not exactly. What it says is that there is no worse punishment than to live out your life in pain.

Jack   How very true, Sir.

Gant   No, Jack, it is a lie. There is far worse than living your life in pain.

Poulet   But what could be worse than that?

Gant   Simple, my dear – living your life without it.

Pause.

Jack   I'm sure you must be right, Sir, but it sounds very wrong.

Ludd   It's drivel, that's why! Another woolly bourgeois fantasy!

Gant   I bow to your great experience, of course. But indulge me for a moment.

Pause.

Let us say that the surgery worked. That the image of his love is gone from his mind. He knows that he loved, and that he lost, but he has no face to embody that loss. The pain is but a notion; it has no effect on his heart.

Jack   I like it, Sir! It is altogether cheerier.

Gant   Wait a moment, Jack. The pain of losing her has gone. But so has the joy of loving her. He remembers his time with her as if it were but a tale, told him by a stranger.

Pause.

Time passes, but he never finds such a love again. He is content, but only that; never angry nor inspired – simply content.

Pause.

Jack   I'm confused. I thought being content was good.

Poulet   But he feels no passion, Jack!

Jack   Oh, right.

Pause.

And that's bad, is it?

Gant   Yes, Jack. Edgar's love for this woman was the defining moment of his life, yet he cannot savour it. He is like a man with no taste buds at the perfect meal.

Jack   Ah. Well, now you put it that way, yes, that would be annoying, to be sure.

Poulet   Is there nothing he can do to reverse the situation?

Gant   Of course.

Pause.

He can remove the cork.

Jack   But that would kill him!

Gant   Indeed. But before he dies, he will see his Louisa's face once more.

Ludd   Sentimental dung!

Poulet   But he cannot do this, Edward. He will have broken his vow to her.

Gant   Exactly. 'If we are to meet again,' she said, 'it must be by God's will alone.'

Poulet   So what will he do?

Gant   What indeed?

Pause.

Jack   I don't see what's wrong with the story as it stands. Let us leave it as it is.

Gant   No, my friend. I meant what I said. There will be no more shows.

Poulet   But why? What will we do with ourselves?

Gant   My sweet Madame Poulet, I have always been fond of you. You are a warm breeze across my heart. I have no doubt that a woman of your beauty and talent will go on to greater things.

Ludd   If not, there's always the egg-laying.

Gant   Exactly. And Jack – my timepiece, my constant – while ever men need decency and valour, there will be a place for you.

Ludd   If not your boring war stories.

Gant   And Nicholas – you have your passion for reality. I suspect you will come to find it misplaced, but then it is the journey, not the arriving.

Pause.

Ludd   Look – I know I've come on a bit strong –

Gant   Hush now. Do not disappoint me.

He turns to the audience.

My good and pure ladies. My brave and gentle men. I hope you will find it in your hearts to excuse our indulgence; and that it is some consolation to have at least been present at an event. Namely, the last ever performance of *The Amazing Feats of Loneliness.*

My name – is Edward Gant!

For the first time, he removes his top hat.

Prodigy! Soldier!

And now we can see –

Traveller! Poet!

– like **Edgar Thomas Dawn**, *he has a cork in his head!*

Gant   But always – and ever – a showman!

And, with this, he removes the cork from his head.

Blood spills down across his face . . .

Sanzonetta – !

He smiles sadly –

Forgive me . . .

– and then collapses to the ground.

Madame Poulet *is the first to go to him, followed by* **Jack**, *who feels for his pulse.*

Ludd   Is he . . . ?

Pause. **Jack** *nods.*

Pause.

Poulet   Take him off! Ludd!

Quickly, **Ludd** *and* **Madame Poulet** *drag* **Gant**'s *corpse off the stage, leaving* **Jack** *alone.*

Jack   Um – ladies and gentlemen –

Pause. The skyhooks lower. On the verge of tears, **Jack** *crosses to the planet Earth and reattaches it to the hooks. He shouts up into the rafters.*

Take up the world!

The world creaks back up into the rafters.

He stares at the audience, searching for the words. He can find only these:

Edward Gant is dead.

And he exits, not quite sure which way to go.

(Note: it is up to you how the curtain call is taken, in character or not. But you might ask yourself whether what we have seen should be taken as truth, or whether it has all been just an artifice created by Gant, ever the showman. The decision is yours.)